ICELAND

The Ultimate Iceland Travel Guide By A Traveler For A Traveler

The Best Travel Tips: Where To Go, What To See And Much More

SECOND EDITION

Table of Contents

Why Lost Travelers Guides?

First, we want to wish you an amazing time in Iceland when you plan to visit. Also we would like to thank you and congratulate you for downloading our travel guide, *"Iceland; The Ultimate Iceland Travel Guide By A Traveler For A Traveler"*.

Allow us to explain our beginnings, and the reason we created Lost Travelers. Lost Travelers was created due to one simple problem that other guides on the market did not solve; loss of time. Considering it's the 21st century and everything is available online, why do we still purchase guidebooks? To save us time! That's right.

Since the goal is to be efficient and save time, we did not understand why there are several guidebooks on the market that are of 500 to 1000 page' long. We do not believe one needs that much bluff to get an overview of the location and some remarkable suggestions. Considering many guidebooks on the market are filled with "suggestions" that were sponsored for, we have decided to take a different approach and provide our travelers with an honest opinion and decline any sort of sponsorship. This simply allows us to cut off any nonsense and create our guides the Lost Travelers style.

Our mission is simple; to create an easy to follow guide book that outlines the best of activities to do in our limited time at the destination. This easily saves you your most valuable asset; your time. You no longer need to spend hours looking through a massive book, or spend hours searching for information on the internet as we have completed the whole process for you. The best part is we provide you our e-guides for one third the price of the leading brand, and our paper copy for only half the price.

Thanks again for choosing us, we hope you enjoy!

Chapter 1: Welcome to Iceland

Overview

Iceland, also known as "The land of Fire and Ice," is a country with extreme geographic make up. While it has some of Europe's largest glaciers, it also has some of the most active volcanoes in the world. Thus, Iceland is also dubbed as the country of light and darkness. During summer, Iceland has nearly 24 hours of sunshine while during winter, it only has few daylight hours.

Although Iceland is ultimately a young country, its traditions are quite old. For instance, in 930 A.D. its oldest parliament, Þingvellir was formed. Today, the site of the   Þingvellir is one of UNESCO'S world heritage sites. Þingvellir is found at the juncture of the continental plates of North America and Eurasia. The juncture, however, is also located in some other areas in Iceland such as the Blue Lagoon.

Iceland has a diverse landscape that changes with through each season. For instance, as you travel in the southwest, you will find moss-covered lava fields. When you drive around in the northwest, you will find soaring fjords.

As mentioned earlier, Iceland is a young country being the last one to settle in Europe. In the 9th and 10th century, emigrants from the British Isles and Scandinavia came to live in the island. On the other hand, Iceland remains to be the continent's most thinly populated country. In fact, for every square meter, you will find less than three inhabitants.

Nature's unrelenting forces bring about the coarse natural environment of Iceland. However, the country has become extremely resilient as it faces extreme conditions. The inhabitants of Iceland have also learned to harness the country's natural resources regardless of these conditions.

The Icelandic culture is founded in the Icelandic language that has bred a literary tradition way back to the ancient Icelandic Sagas. In this modern age, this strong literary tradition still flourishes as most authors from Iceland publish more books as compared to any other country across the globe. In addition, Iceland also boasts of its music scene, Icelandic design, and film industry.

The traditions and customs of Iceland are based on its history of insular existence as well as a mixed influence of paganism and Christian doctrine. Furthermore, an arduous environment and the natural resources shape Icelandic folk tales. These tales often include ghosts, mysticism, elves, and even trolls.

Brief History

In the late 9th century A.D., the first Viking settlers came to Iceland, which they found to be empty. While Iceland is known today as a modern country, it still carries the evidence of its cultural heritage.

The settlement period is said to have held persisted for about 60 years in which all lands that are inhabitable were claimed. In circa 30,000, Iceland's population was 30,000.

- ### *Age of the Vikings*

Most of the settlers in Iceland came from Norway. They emigrated due to socio-economic and political factors. Other settlers came from Sweden and Denmark. Some came from the British Isles.

Based on the modern Icelander DNA analysis, about 60% of female settlers have Celtic origins. It is said that slaves from the Norse settlers are likely to have Celtic origins as well.

- ### *The Alþingi Parliament*

The early Icelandic society had no head of state or king, but only organized on a regional basis. Local assemblies were held to discuss and resolve important matters as well as disputes.

In 930 A.D., the National Assembly or Commonwealth, better known as the Alþingi was founded and established as a common law. Every month of June, local chieftains along with their followers met annually at Þingvellir where legal cases were done and legislation was passed. The assembly was also a form of trade forum and social gathering.

- ### *Medieval Iceland*

Medieval Iceland was primarily a farming society where temporary or seasonal settlements flourish at fishing posts or trading sites. During this period, the society was purely rural. There were no towns or villages.

The settlers built farms, which were established using the available natural resources such as drift wood, turf, forested timber, and stone. During the early settlement period, the medieval sources were thickly-wooded. For instance, a typical farm construction would include a main log house and several outhouses with a common hall wherein farm members lived.

The medieval daily life was controlled by the seasons; thus, the farms were self-sustaining. Iceland's average temperature was warmer during the settlement period, which made it possible to crop rye, barley, and oats. The settlers brought farm animals with them including goats, poultry, cows, pigs, and sheep. They also had domestic animals such as horses and dogs. The diet during the medieval period was meat and dairy based with occasional fish. During autumn, meat from animals was soured in whey or smoked while fish was dried.

- **Iceland 1500 - 1800**

16th century Iceland, just as the rest of Europe, saw a massive change in society and religious beliefs. During the 1530s, the country converted to Protestantism and in 1539, the Danish king ordered that the church's land in Iceland was to be confiscated. However, the bishops of Iceland refused to hand over the land and two years later, the Danish king sent an army to take it by force. Eventually, a new bishop was placed in Skalholt but the bishop of Holar, named Jon Aranson, remained steadfast in his refusal to back down. In addition to being a bishop, he was also a strong chieftain with influence amongst his soldiers and support from his two sons, conceived by his concubine. In 1548, Aranson was proclaimed to be an outlaw; in retaliation, his men were able to capture the Protestant bishop but two years later, Aranson and his sons were caught and executed. After this, the people slowly accepted the new religion and in 1584, the Bible was first translated into the native language.

During the 17th century, things began to get hard for the Icelandic people. In 1602, the king issued a new decree that only particular merchants in Elsinore, Copenhagen and Malmo would have control of trade with Iceland. In 1619, this network of merchants was made a joint stock company. For the Icelanders, this meant that they had no choice but to sell at rock bottom prices and purchase from them at extremely high prices. As can be imagined, the economy in Iceland was completely damaged.

In 1661, the Danish king proclaimed himself the ruler of all. By the next year, Iceland had no choice but to suffer his complete rule over them. The Althing would still come together but by this time, they had severely lost all their power. Between 1707 – 1709, smallpox broke out over the island and wiped out a large portion of the population.

During the mid-18th century, a man named Skuli Magnusson was made a fogd, an official, who then attempted to turn the economy around. To start with, he brought in farmers from Norway and Denmark, and then he had improved fishing boats created before establishing a wool industry using weavers from Germany in the Reykjavik. In 1787, the Danish merchant's control was finally at an end.

However, at this time, Iceland's population was at an estimated 38,000 people due to volcanic eruptions. In 1800, the Althing met for the last time, replaced by a new, modern court at Reykjavik, when the town's population was at around 300 people.

- ## 19th Century Iceland

The relationship between Denmark and Iceland deteriorated during the 19th century. At this time, the concept of nationalism was spreading throughout Europe, including Iceland. We can see this in the song, O Guo vors land, which was produced in 1874.

In 1843, the Danish king recalled the Althing, which met for the first time again two years later but it no longer held any real power. Nationalism continued to spread throughout the country and in 1874, Christian IX proclaimed a new constitution but though it was under the Althing, it didn't have a lot of influence. In 1904, the role of governor was ended and Iceland was allowed to rule themselves.

In 1854, Iceland was finally permitted to trade with other countries and the fishing industry improved and grew in the latter part of the 19th century due to the new sailing ships instead of the traditional rowing boats.

- ## 20th Century Iceland

In 1911, Reykjavik University was established, Iceland's economy improved, the population increased even with a mass emigration to Canada, and in 1918, Iceland was declared a sovereign state that shared a king with Denmark. Women were given the right to vote in 1915, with the first woman entering the Althing seven years later.

In May 1940, British soldiers invaded Iceland but the Icelanders were helped by the United States. Four years later, Iceland finally broke free from the Danish monarchy, becoming an independent country. In 1947, a volcano erupted, resulting in much devastation. Two years later, Iceland became a member of NATO.

The Cod Wars between Iceland and the United Kingdom came about from the 1950s to the 1970s. Iceland was becoming scared that the British were over-fishing but were finally resolved in 1976. The first female elected president in the world was done in Iceland during the 1980s.

- **21st Century Iceland**

There have been a number of innovations in 21st century Iceland. First, they began using the natural hot water they used for keeping their houses warm, to heat their greenhouses. The Unites States of America declared they would be removing their armed forces from the country.

In 2008, the top three banks in Iceland failed, causing an economic crisis of epic proportions, with ramifications all over the world. The following year, the government fell due to widespread demonstrations and unemployment figures rose to more than nine percent.

Today's estimated population in Iceland sits at around 331,000 and the standard of living is good.

Location, Geography, and Climate

Iceland is found in the westernmost part of Europe. It is a North Atlantic island, which lies about 970 kilometers west of Norway and 800 kilometers northwest of Scotland. Iceland's northern coast is found directly below the Arctic Circle. Its capital is the Reykjavík, which is located in the northernmost part of the world.

Iceland is a huge island located in the Atlantic Ocean and near the Arctic Circle. An island called Grímsey found in the country's northern part has half of its landmass lying within the Arctic Circle. It would take three hours to fly from London to Reykjavík and five hours from New York.

Following the Great Britain, Iceland is Europe's second largest island. It stretches across 40,000 square miles of 103,000 km2, which is almost the same size as Portugal and Hungary or Virginia and Kentucky.

Iceland's widest parts measures 305 miles from east to west and 185 miles from north to south. Its coastline is about 4,970 kilometers. The country maintains an exclusive economic zone of about 200 nautical miles. With a 10-day holiday, you can drive around the island's coastal route.

Most of the terrain of Iceland consists of mountain peaks, plateaus, and fertile lowlands, which may be one of the reasons why 80% of it remains uninhabited. Iceland has a number of glaciers and fjords, including the Vatnajökull, Europe's largest glacier. Volcanoes, geysers, steaming lava fields, black sand beaches, and waterfalls define the country's landscape.

Iceland is one of the world's youngest landmasses and also home of some of the most active volcanoes across the globe. The existence of Iceland is due to a volcanic hotspot brought about by a crack in the Mid-Atlantic ridge in which the American and Eurasian tectonic plates adjoin.

The landmass continues to grow each year by about 5 cm, splitting wider at its points where the tectonic plates adjoin. The Eyjafjallajökull and the Grímsvötn volcanoes were the last to erupt in 2010 and 2011 respectively. Iceland also has the newest island in the world known as Surtsey, which was formed in 1063 through a volcanic eruption.

Climate

If you are in Iceland and you find that you do not favor the weather, all you need to do is wait for five minutes until the weather changes. The Gulf Stream is said to cause this abrupt change. Thus, you can enjoy a temperate maritime climate, fairly mild winters, and refreshing summers during your visit to Iceland. In addition, the East Greenland polar current also affects Icelandic weather as it curves southeastwards going around the east and north coasts. Consequently, the abrupt changes in weather are common in which travelers and visitors should be prepared for.

Culture

As mentioned earlier, Iceland is the youngest country in Europe, being the last to get settled. Upon the arrival of the Viking settlers during the late 9th century, they found an island, which is uninhabited. During the 10th century, emigrants from the British Isles and Scandinavia settled in the country.

The location of Iceland made it an isolated country of fishermen and farmers until the dawn of the 20th century. The extreme nature and isolation have molded the country's culture, causing it to become resilient. The Icelandic family ties are strong and their sense of tradition is firm. Furthermore, inhabitants of the country have a powerful bond with nature.

Through the years, Iceland has established a unique tradition for literature as well as storytelling. This began with the reputable Icelandic Sagas during the 10th and 11th centuries. For years, Icelandic literature and storytelling were passed down orally; however, during the 13th and 14th centuries, they were already published in paper.

The Icelandic language from the old Sagas was preserved carefully. In fact, the country's language is the least changed among the Nordic countries. This is due to the island's long-time agenda of the government to preserve the language as well as protect it from external influences. A committee in the government functions efficiently to establish unique Icelandic terminology for new things, including "sjónvarp" for television or TV. The committee works in creating such terminology instead of incorporating borrowed words into the Icelandic language. In addition, the isolation of the island from mainland Europe helps in preserving its language.

Language

The national language of the country is Icelandic. Most Icelanders speak English, being the official second language, which is taught in schools. Its official third language is Danish, which is also taught in Icelandic schools.

Basic Information

- *When driving in Iceland*

The Ring Road Nr.1 courses through island and is about 827 miles. In urban areas, the general speed limit is up to 50 km/h. In rural areas, the speed limit is 80 km/h on gravel roads and 90 km/h on asphalt roads.

There is a loose gravel surface in all roads in Iceland's interior and mountain roads. When driving in this surface, you should be extra careful as it is specifically loose along the sides of the roads. Mountain roads are not constructed for speeding as they are narrow.

- *When shopping in Iceland*

The good news: if you plan to shop in Iceland is that it is tax-free. You can refund the value added tax (VAT) on all your purchases upon request as long as it exceeds 6000 ISK. VAT is already included in the prices of items. It is collected in two brackets depending on the items purchased or services availed. For instance, VAT refund will be 20% if the item or service falls in the higher bracket (24%) or 10% if the item or service falls in the lower bracket (11%). The maximum refund is 15% of the items' retail price.

- *What to wear in Iceland*

Travelers should be prepared for the abrupt changes in weather when in Iceland. For instance, it is advisable to bring a cardigan, sweater, or lightweight woolens. It is also best to bring weatherproof or rainproof coat and a comfortable pair of walking shoes. If you plan to camp, it is advisable to bring warm socks and underwear, a warm sleeping bag, and a pair of rubber boots.

- *Icelandic Regulations for Passport and Visa*

Iceland honors the Schengen Agreement that exempts visitors from personal border control in 22 European countries. Residents of countries, which are outside the Schengen area need a valid pass for the duration of their stay. It is best to visit the Icelandic Directorate of Immigration website to know more about the Schengen area regulations and other requirements for passport and visa.

- *Icelandic Mobile Service*

The code to use when calling into Iceland from overseas is 354 plus the seven-digit number. If you are in Iceland, you can make long-distance calls to the USA and Europe by dialing 00 plus the country code with the telephone number. There are four major GSM service providers in Iceland, including Vodafone, Nova, Siminn, and TAL. These services provide cover for most parts of the island, including areas that are unpopulated. Pre-paid GSM phone cards are also available from these service providers. You can also avail of credit refill cards from convenience stores and gas stations in Iceland.

For Internet connection, you can rent a portable iPad or WiFi at Trawire. This way, you can connect to the Internet at an unlimited usage and fixed price. The portable iPad or WiFi can accommodate up to 10 mobile devices via 3G and 4G without changing the SIM card of your own mobile device. Laptops can also connect to this portable gadget.

- ***Emergency Numbers***

Emergency number:	112
Police:	444-1000
Medical assistance:>	1770
Dental emergency:	575-0505
Information:	1819
Telegrams:	1446
Alcoholics Anonymous:	551-2010

Chapter 2: East Coast of Iceland

Iceland's east coast boasts of its lush farmlands, largest forest, and a series of small islands and fjords. The east coast is also home to a number of natural harbors, small seaside communities, and fishing villages, which border the coast.

In the eastern coast of Iceland, travelers will be amazed with its impressive chambers of magma, which are filled with colorful mineral deposits. During summer, the east coast becomes a center for young people and artists both from Iceland and abroad. A number of art and music festivals pops up in the eastern coast. In fact, this has become a tradition that expands steadily each year.

If you are coming from Europe via the Smyril Line ferry, your landing area will be in Seyðisfjörður. With its 19th century village as a backdrop, Seyðisfjörður is home to an emerging art scene in this part of Iceland.

The landscape in the East has a rich history of art and palette. Icelandic painter, Jóhannes Sveinsson Kjarval, one of the most popular artists of Iceland, grew up in the Eastern town of Borgarfjörður eystri. In this town, Kjarval created several of his most memorable pieces of work. Furthermore, a museum is now built in this town to commemorate the life and work of the painter.

Indeed, Iceland's east coast boasts of interesting music and arts festivals that usually run throughout the year.

How to Get to the East Coast of Iceland

- *Flights*

WOW Air and Iceland Air are operating flights to Iceland from North America and Europe. The international airport is located in Keflavík, which is around 40 to 50 minutes away from Iceland's capital, Reykjavík.

Through plane, you can reach the east coast via Air Iceland, which offers 3 to 5 flights daily from Reykjavík to East Iceland's Egilsstaðir.

- *Ferry*

The Norræna ferry sails weekly to and from Denmark all the way to Seyðisfjörður in East Iceland. It has one stopover in Faroe Islands.

The ferry that sails between Norðfjörður and Mjóifjörður operates twice a week during wintertime, which is from October 1 to May 31. It sails on Mondays and Thursdays at 10:00 a.m. from Mjóifjörður and back from Norðfjörður at 12:30 p.m.

- *Buses*

There are a few bus operators that you can take when traveling to the east coast of Iceland. These include SV-Aust., Strætó BS, and SBA-Norðurleið/Sterna. SV-Aust. operates in East Iceland all year round. Its stops include Seyðisfjörður, Reyðarfjörður, Fáskrúðsfjörður, Breiðdalsvík, Höfn,

Borgarfjörður, Eskifjörður, Stöðvarfjörður, Egilsstaðir, Djúpivogur, and Neskaupstaður.

Strætó BS operates in East Iceland via Route 56 all year round. Its path is from Egilsstaðir to Akureyri and vice versa. During summer, it operates daily while during winter, it operates 3 to 5 times a week.

SBA-Norðurleið/Sterna probably has the most number of circuits in East Iceland. It offers day tours and bus passport system. It travels from Akureyri to Egilsstaðir to Höfn and vice versa. From June 1 to September 10, SBA-Norðurleið's route62A is from Höfn - Egilsstadir - Myvatn - Akureyri and vice versa.

- **Car**

You can drive via a car rental from Iceland's capital, Reykjavik to Egilsstaðir in just one day. You can take either the northern or southern route.

- **Taxi**

If you are in Egilsstaðir and in need of a taxi service, you can contact the following: Jón Eiður Jónsson, with phone number 892-9247 and e-mail joneidur@gmail.com; Jón Björnsson with phone number 898-2625 and e-mail sputnik@simnet.is; and Guttormur Kristmannsson with phone number 659 4828.

If you are in Reyðarfjörður, you can contact Gunnar Th Gunnarsson with phone number 844-9133.

If you are in Eskifjörður, you can contact Sturlaugur Stefánsson with phone number 852-2227 or Bjarni Hávarðsson with phone number 893-3450.

Where to Go in East Iceland

- ## *Skaftfell – Center for Visual Art*

Skaftfell is known as a center for contemporary art, showcasing various activities, events, exhibitions, and educational programs both on a local and international degree. Apart from offering various activities and programs, Skaftfell boasts of its bistro, which serves delectable food, coffee, and other beverages. It also offers an art library with free Internet connection.

Skaftfell is home of a minuscule house, which was owned previously by Ásgeir Emilsson, a local naïve artist. This minuscule house can only be viewed upon request.

- ## *Auroras Iceland*

If you came to Iceland to enjoy the northern lights exhibition, you can visit the Wathne's House, which showcases one of a kind photo called "Dance with the Mountains" by Jónína and Jóhanna. The photo exhibits the majestic mountains in Fáskrúðsfjörður, which circle the fjord, letting you experience the northern lights. It is open from 12:00 noon to 10:00 in the evening from May 15 to September 30.

Incidentally, The Icelandic House of the Northern Lights located in a small village in Iceland's eastern coast will open in August 2018. There, you will have a better view of the northern lights. Until that time, you can visit the Wathne's House.

- *Randulffs-Sjóhús*

Situated by the sea in Eskifjördur, Randulff's Sea House opens during the months of summer, serving dinner with a traditional local menu. It is available for reservation specifically for those who come in groups. Randulff's Sea House is open from 12 noon to 10 in the evening daily during summer months. The menu is primarily comprised of fresh, local ingredients.

The building of the restaurant is elegantly preserved as the old house it used to be. It is home to several artifacts and provides an atmosphere from the days when herring fishery initiated the real growth of East Iceland's fjord towns during the lat 19th century and early 20th century.

- **Local culture and summit hikes in Seyðisfjörður**

While the main international route into East Iceland is at Egilsstaðir, there is a ferry service that connects the country with Denmark and the Faroe Islands at Seyðisfjörður. The Symril Line can be found at this stunning little town, situated on Route 93. Seyðisfjörður used to be a key ferring port town in the past, with its vibrantly coloured wooden houses constructed by merchants. Today, it is a popular destination for artists, with a number of the houses being transformed into stores selling arts and crafts. Visitors can browse for souvenirs before enjoying live music at Blaa Kirkjan, also known as the Blue Church, during the summer months. Head up the hills and explore the stunning scenery, which includes cascading waterfalls and a lake that freezes over. For adrenaline junkies, kayaking and mountain biking is on offer. Seyðisfjörður was recently used as the backdrop for the crime drama, *Trapped*.

- **Fish and Yoga**

Seyðisfjörður isn't the only town in east Iceland to enjoy fame. In Reyðarfjörður, which also can be found along Route 92, was used in the TV drama *Fortitude*. Visitors can still see the faux storefronts and signposts all in the Norwegian language lined in this charming town. Carry on along the coastline and you'll discover the picture-perfect town of Stöðvarfjörður. Not long ago, it suffered greatly as the fishing industry declined but the local residents have transformed it into the Fish Factory – a colony of artists that includes a music studio.

For visitors who wish to explore and discover more about East Iceland, head to Breiðdalsvík. This sleepy little town hosts Tinna Adventure, a company that allows visitors to explore the region. Discover hidden gems such as waterfalls, or head out to sea and watch puffins and fishing opportunities. It's also known for its yoga – practice on top of a hill overlooking the town as you breath in and out – an experience not to be missed.

- **Slow Things Down in Djúpivogur**

Head to the southernmost part of East Iceland and discover the peaceful port town of **Djúpivogur**, the nearest of its kind to the rest of Europe. In the past, the town was home to wool merchants from Germany and pirates from North Africa. However, today you will find it a relaxing and quiet place, with no adverts proclaiming its recent Slow City award. It features an up-scale restaurant within Hotel Framtid and a store renowned for its items used by locally sourced materials, including leather made from lambs, reindeer pelts and fish skin. Explore the local region – it boasts endless obsidian-hued beaches and boat trips to see native wildlife.

Nightlife in East Iceland

Nightlife in East Iceland is not the heart-pumping action you may find in other countries, but there are still places to enjoy.

- **Kaffi Egilsstaoir**

Located in Egilsstadir, Kaffi Egilsstadir looks nondescript at first glance, but head inside to enjoy cheap beer and a comfortable atmosphere with friendly staff and locals. The bar also serves a good range of foods to sample.

- **Hotel Aldan**

Situated in Seydisfjordur, Hotel Aldan is the best bet for tasty salmon dishes but their bar serves a good range of beverages. Occasionally, they host live musical performances.

Where to Eat in East Iceland

- ## *Hja Okkur*

Housed in Síreksstaðir, which is a traditional farm breeding goats, hens, rabbits, sheep, horses, and ducks, the restaurant, Hja Okkur serves an exquisite menu comprised of local ingredients. It offers authentic Icelandic food that travelers should not miss when visiting East Iceland.

- ## *Cafe Nielsen*

This restaurant and cafe is located in Egilsstaðir's oldest house. It offers a wide variety of menu, including meat, fish, and vegetables among others. Its house specialty is the popular reindeer steak. Cafe Nielsen also serves chocolate, coffee, and cakes that will truly make visitors come back for more. It has a lunch buffet, which is available during weekdays from 11:30 a.m. to 1:30 p.m. One of the most favorite spot in the restaurant is its veranda where travelers can spend the late afternoon.

Where to Stay in East Iceland

Kaffihúsið Guesthouse is situated in one of Eskifjörður's small fishing village, which is known for beautifully preserved red herring sea lodges circling the coast. Kaffihúsið Guesthouse is near Helgustaðanáma and the Gerpir area; thus, travelers can enjoy the great trails of coves and falls. Apart from staying in the guesthouse, travelers can also enjoy its restaurant serving authentic Icelandic dishes. Another treat that the guesthouse offers is the Harðskafi, which is the famous mountain side mentioned in most of the best-selling novels by Arnaldur Indriðason.

Kaffihúsið Guesthouse is said to have a cozy atmosphere, making it a home away from home. It provides a professional yet personal service to its guests, attending to their individual needs.

Kaffihúsið Guesthouse has 11 rooms with 5 single and 6 double rooms. Each room has washbasins as well as flat screen television. Breakfast is also served in its restaurant. Those interested to stay in the Kaffihúsið Guesthouse can visit its website www.kaffihusid.is for booking.

- ***Hotel Tangi***

Situated in the center of the Vopnafjordur town, Hotel Tangi offers 4 rooms, each with a television and a private bath. There is also one room available for disabled persons. Travelers can enjoy the friendly and welcoming atmosphere of the hotel. A sitting area with a television, bar, and restaurant is situated on the ground floor. Hotel Tangi's restaurant opens from 7:00 a.m. to 10 a.m. for breakfast and from 6:00 p.m. to

9:00 p.m. for dinner. The hotel also has 13 double rooms on its upper floor each with washbasins although showers and washrooms are shared.

- ### *Hotel Edda Egilsstadir (Eastern Promise)*

Hotel Edda Egilsstadir is located in Egilsstaðir, which is dubbed as the "capital of the east." The hotel is near the international airport as well as a number of East Iceland's local attractions, including the extinct Mount Snæfell volcano, the Hallormsstaður (Iceland's largest forest), the Lagarfljót river, and the sandy cove of Atlavík's.

Hotel Edda Egilsstadir boasts of its 52 rooms, all are en-suite. It also has split-level family rooms, a restaurant with magnificent views of the river, meeting and conference rooms, a paddling pool, golf (9 holes), and a 25-meter open-air swimming pool.

The hotel also offers glacier and mountain tours, seal spotting, woodland walks, and bird watching for travelers and visitors looking for activities.

Interested parties can contact the hotel prior to visit to book, arrange car rentals, and/or arrange the available adventures through www.hoteledda.is.

- ### *Hildibrand Hotel*

This hotel is one of the newest boutique apartment hotels in East Iceland. It is located in the center of the Neskaupstaður town, which is a peaceful and majestic fishing village in Nordfjörður. The Hildibrand Hotel offers self-catering apartments that are spacious and all with a private balcony with the views of the fjord. Travelers and visitors can also enjoy the views of the calm waters and majestic mountains while staying in the hotel.

A seafood bistro, sushi, and grill restaurant called Kaupfélagsbarinn is located in the hotel. Travelers and visitors can dine and eat high-quality food with locally-sourced ingredients. The restaurant is decorated elegantly and has a good view of the fjord as well. Travelers and visitors can sit and relax while enjoying the sumptuous food and views.

Interested parties can contact the hotel through a phone call +3544771950 or send an email at hildibrand@hildibrand.com.

What to Do in East Iceland

- *Skiing*

Skiing is among the great outdoor activities that East Iceland offers. Travelers and visitors can try out cross country skiing in the fjords or highlands, ski boarding in various resorts, or sliding on skis with a beautiful scenery.

Oddsskarð is one of Iceland's famous skiing areas, being the largest in East Iceland. It has three lifts, which can accommodate 2,000 people per hour. It also has a ski lodge that has sleeping bag accommodation for over 30 persons. Tracks are also available for cross-country skiing. While enjoying the view of the calm fjords, travelers and visitors can stay on the cafeteria.

Oddsskarð is open in winter from 2:00 p.m. to 8:00 p.m. during weekdays. On weekends, it opens from 10 in the morning until 4 in the afternoon as long as snow is available.

- *Cave Exploring*

Iceland has a number of caves ranging from small to large, shallow to deep, which potholers and spelunkers can explore. Caves can either be explored with or without a guide.

Mjóeyri is one of East Iceland's travel services that provide exploration activities as well as accommodations for travelers and visitors. It is located in Eskifjörður town. The building was originally a family house established in 1895. Mjóeyri was refurbished and preserved to provide warmth, comfort, and an atmosphere of yesteryear.

Mjóeyri provides a magnificent view of Reyðarfjörður and Eskifjörður fjords as well as some surrounding mountains. It offers breakfast and dinner for travelers and visitors who ordered ahead of their visit. It also has five rooms with a living room, joint cooking facilities, and washroom. Each room has a television and radio.

The premises of Mjóeyri are strictly a no-smoking area. There is also a veranda, which leads to sleeping bag accommodations with washroom and cooking facilities. Cottages, each with a veranda and majestic view are also available. Each cottage can accommodate six to seven people. The living rooms of each cottage include a couch, which can be converted into a queen-sized bed. The upper floors of the cottage house a room with an attic and a double bed, which can accommodate 2 to 3 persons. Cottages have Internet access.

Mjóeyri also offers a bathhouse with showers, sauna, and toilets. In front of the bathhouse is a Jacuzzi situated in a boat.

- *Zoo and Farm Activities*

There are various indoor and outdoor parks, zoos, and farms in most parts of Iceland where families can bond and enjoy. One of them is the Icelandic Farm Holidays.

This farm has been around for more than 30 years. It is an award-winning facility specifically for rural activities. It offers guided tours, day tours, and self-drive packages all through the year. It provides an extensive accommodation of country hotels, self-catering cottages, bed and breakfasts, and traditional farms not only in the eastern coast, but all around Iceland.

Local farmers established the Icelandic Farm Holidays in 1980. In fact, majority of travel agency is still owned by the same farmers who founded it. The Icelandic Farm Holidays also promotes tourism through its world-class facilities and activities.

Interested parties can contact the agency for accommodation and booking for a memorable Icelandic holiday.

Chapter 3: West Iceland

One of the most geologically diverse regions of the Icelandic territory is West Iceland. It represents almost all the natural wonders of the country, including majestic waterfalls, slumberous volcanoes, and a variety of wildlife and plant life.

West Iceland is an Icelandic region that is rich in nature, history, and culture complementing each other and resulting to an unforgettable experience. The vast Icelandic region boasts of valleys, glaciers, craters, volcanoes, and fjords. Travelers and visitors can experience great hikes around Hvalfjörður and Akranes or simply marvel at the beauty of Iceland's highest waterfall, Glymur and the majestic mountain, Akrafjall, which are less than an hour away from the country's capital, Reykjavík.

West Iceland is also home to a few famous writers. Travelers and visitors can visit the abode of Snorri Sturluson, a medieval writer in Reykholt and get to see its man-made geothermal bath where the writer often gather his thoughts. Travelers can also learn about Egill Skalla-Grímsson, who was Viking poet known for his awe-inspiring literary work.

There are a number of interesting sites found all around West Iceland in which travelers can marvel at nature and connect it to various stories of the people in the region. History is all over West Iceland as well as marvelous wildlife and landscape. For instance, the region boasts of Iceland's only national park, which meets the sea. This park is known as the Snæfellsjökull National Park. The mystical Snæfellsjökull Glacier volcano is also found in the western region where most poets and artists get inspiration. This volcano is one of the world's greatest energy centers. In addition, Snæfellsjökull is the setting of the "Journey to the Center of the Earth" by Jules Verne.

A city in West Iceland called Snæfellsnes was given an Earth Check award for its beautiful nature as well as being a sustainable local area. Not so far from Snæfellsnes is Dalir, which is the home of some great explorers, including Eirík the Red and Leif the Lucky. They are a European father and son tandem who were first to set foot in America.

Given that there are only short distances between interesting tourist destinations, travelers and visitors are able to enjoy the region all year round at a relaxed and gratifying pace.

Transportation

Travelers and visitors can opt to drive, walk, take a bus, or cycle around West Island. They can even fly through various airlines operating all around the country. In west Island, ferries, car rentals, bus tours, and public transportation are conveniently available for travelers and visitors

Where to Go in West Iceland

- ## *Akranes' Lighthouses*

Travelers and visitors who are into photography or simply like exploring in Iceland can enjoy the most picturesque lighthouses in Akranes. Two lighthouses are situated down the harbor. The bigger of the two lighthouses is open to the public and currently being used. Thus, travelers and visitors can enjoy the view from the lighthouse. A photography exhibition is also offered in the lighthouse.

- ## *Deildartunguhver Hot Spring*

Deildartunguhver hot spring is one of the most powerful hot springs in Europe, with the highest hot water flow of 180 l/sec of 100°C. In fact, most of its water is being used for central heating in some towns, including Akranes and Borgarnes. Akranes' hot water pipeline is about 64 kilometers long, which is the longest in the country. When the water reaches Akranes, it is about 78 to 80 degrees. Travelers and visitors who take a shower within a 65-kilometer radius of the spring have already experienced bathing in the hot water of Deildartunguhver.

- ## *Glymur Waterfall*

Glymur waterfall is the highest waterfall in Iceland. It is situated in the Botnsdalur valley in Hvalfjörður. Travelers and visitors who are into hiking can find a fabulous path although one should not be afraid of challenging hikes or heights. Hikers can expect to reach the top of the path in 3 to 4 hours. On the other hand, it is advisable to hike in the Glymur waterfall during summer, as it can be quite difficult to hike during winter when the path is cold and icy.

- ### *Langjökull Glacier*

Langjökull is the second largest glacier in Europe. It has caves and an ice tunnel where travelers and visitors can explore the glacier from the inside. The ice cave only opened last June of 2015. One will find the experience one of a kind, as the hidden beautiful ice is truly mesmerizing.

- ### *Snæfellsjökull Glacier*

The Snæfellsjökull glacier is said to be the center of the Earth. It is located 1446m above sea level. It is an active volcano, which was established through a number of eruptions. Most people in this side of Iceland that the glacier is one of the Earth's seven main energy centers and considered by many as mystical. The novel of Jules Verne called "The Center of the Earth" written in 1864 used the glacier as its setting. Snæfellsjökull glacier is one of the highlights of the Snæfellsjökull National Park. The purposes of the park are to conserve and protect the areas, including the animal life, indigenous plants, historical relics, and the unique landscape of Snæfellsjökull. The park also serves as the easiest access to the glacier.

Where to Eat in West Iceland

- ### *Munaðarnes Restaurant*

This restaurant is a cozy and friendly restaurant situated in the center of the Saga land. It offers a sumptuous menu, including lobster soup, salmon, lamb, small dishes, and hamburgers among others. Travelers and visitors can enjoy the great atmosphere of the restaurant, which also has a bar, a playground for children, mini-golf, and a small football pitch. WiFi access is also available in the restaurant. It is open daily from May 15 to September 30 from 10 in the morning until 9 in the evening.

- ### *Bjargarsteinn Mathús (House of Food)*

Bjargarsteinn House of Food is one of the new restaurants in West Iceland situated in an old structure on the seaside. Apart from its menu that changes according the chef's choice and the season, guest can enjoy good service as well as a marvelous view of the Grundafjörður fjord and Mt. Kirkjufell. Bjargarsteinn Restaurant is a family-run business headed by Gunnar Garðarson, a professional chef with highly competent experience.

Where to Stay in West Iceland

- ## *Hotel Fransiskus*

This hotel has 21 rooms, which are designed with a cozy atmosphere and soft, relaxing colors. There are single, double, and family rooms available, each with a magnificent view of the town center, the harbor, the Breiðafjörður bay, and the mountains. Each room is also equipped with the latest amenities. The Hotel Fransiskus was formerly a Catholic monastery. Today, it still has a chapel inside, which is open to the public. Nuns of St. Mary's go to the chapel daily to pray.

Interested parties may visit their website www.fransiskus.is for booking and inquiries.

- ## *Hotel Framnes*

Hotel Framnes is originally a fishermen's hotel in 154 given that it is located alongside of the sea. Although it has undergone a couple of renovations to provide a cozier and warmer atmosphere, guests can still experience a feeling of the past. It is located in Grundafjörður, which is considered as the center of the peninsula of Snæfellsnes. Given that Grundafjörður is a small fishing village and a central locality, Hotel Framnes is a perfect place for travelers and visitors to stay. It would only take a few minutes to go to interesting attractions on the peninsula of Snæfellsnes.

In the main building, Hotel Framnes offers 29 bright yet comfortable rooms equipped with private bathrooms. In the new annex building, there are 8 budget hotels, also with private bathrooms. The annex building is about 50 meters away from the main building.

Each room offered in Hotel Framnes has a television, hairdryer, and coffee/tea facilities. The hotel also has accessible WiFi for guests throughout the vicinity. Rooms that face the west have the magnificent view of the Hell's Gate Mountain, which bosoms the village. The rooms facing the east have a magnificent view of the sea as well as the fjord. In addition, guest can enjoy bird watching while in the comfort of their rooms.

Hotel Framnes has an outdoor hot tub and sauna for guests who want to unwind after a tiring day. The hot tub provides a marvelous view of the sea to the delight of guests. The restaurant in Hotel Framnes can accommodate up to 60 guests. It is located on the ground floor of the main building. The restaurant offers Icelandic lamb, chicken, and gourmet seafood, which is its specialty. The house chef has also created vegetarian dishes. The restaurant is open daily from April 20 to September 30 although it may open during winter months upon request.

Interested parties may contact the hotel for booking and prices via their website www.hotelframnes.is

- **Hotel Glymur**

Hotel Glymur is one of the most popular boutique hotels in West Iceland. It has 25 executive rooms, 6 luxury villas, and 2 superior luxury suites. Executive rooms have two floors and equipped with a sitting room and a bathroom on the lower floor and a sleeping area on the upper room.

All rooms in the Hotel Glymur have flat screen television with about 10 channels, a coffee machine, telephone, a hairdryer, and wireless Internet access.

The two superior luxury suites are the Hallgrímsstofa and the Guðríðarstofa. The Hallgrímsstofa is quite a huge room (46 square meters) with a 28-inch television in the living room and a 20-inch flat screen television in the bedroom. The beds with massage are adjustable. The Hallgrímsstofa suite, which is named after a famous poet of the 16th century who lived in the church near the hotel, is also equipped with a stereo and an espresso machine.

The Guðríðarstofa suite is named after the poet's wife. It is a 37 square meter suite equipped with a 20-inch flat screen television, a massage bathtub, espresso machine, stereo, and adjustable beds with massage.

The luxury villas of the Hotel Glymur have bedrooms, open space kitchen, and bathrooms with the latest appliances. Each villa is equipped with a large screen television, beautiful art pieces with unique themes, dining table, and leather sofas. The dining area of each villa can accommodate 4 to 6 guests. The villas also have spacious bedrooms with huge design beds, fine leather chairs and tables, nightstands and chests, and flat screen televisions. The villas have outdoor Jacuzzis, which is accessible via the bathrooms. The accommodations in the villas include bed linen, bathroom towels and ropes, and daily maintenance. There are also sunny verandas in each villa, which are equipped with outdoor furniture and hot thermal Jacuzzis.

All hotel rooms, suites, and villas have phone access, room service, and catering from the Hotel Glymur restaurant and bar. In addition, the hotel has available outdoor hot tubs and conference facilities. Hotel Glymur is decorated with a special art collection and has a small gift shop in the lobby.

The Hotel Glymur restaurant and bar offers authentic Icelandic culinary art, which includes a wide range of gourmet dishes. An added bonus when guests dine in the restaurant is the breathtaking views. The restaurant serves set menus, á la Carte, and buffets for individuals and groups. The hotel's coffee shop, Café Glymur, is open everyday from 1 p.m. to 5 p.m.

Interested parties may contact the hotel for prices and booking via their website www.hotelglymur.is

What to Do in West Iceland

- ## *Bjarnarhöfn Shark Museum*

For families and groups, the Bjarnarhöfn Shark Museum is a perfect place to go. It provides a variety of exhibits and information about the shark. It also offers travelers and visitors the chance to learn how sharks are handled. The museum also offers Icelandic tobacco, tequila, and Brennivín in its small restaurant.

- ## *Whale Watching*

One of the best times to see whales in the western side of Iceland is during winter. In Grundafjörður, whales are visible during winter months especially if travelers and visitors avail of the Orca trips.

- ## *4x4 Bike Tours*

Travelers and visitors who want to experience a different adventure can try driving an ATV or Quad in the snow. They can take a ride at the Þórisstöðum and drive up to the mountains. They can also enjoy the magnificent view of the Hvalfjörður once they reach the high parts of the mountains via the bike tour.

- ## Akranes' Lighthouses

Akranes Lighthouses are probably one of the most iconic lighthouses in the world, let alone just Iceland. There are two lighthouses close to the harbour in Akranes. Sat the moment, only the larger lighthouse is open for use by the public. Climb all the way to the top of the lighthouse and enjoy panoramic views across the coastline. Head back downstairs and marvel at the photos within the photograph exhibition here.

- **Breiðafjörður**

Breiðafjörður boasts an estimated 3,000 islands and islets scattered across the coastline. One of the most popular islands to visit here is Flately, home to various geothermal attractions, including the iconic basalt columns. This area is home to 50% of the country's intertidal, where the tides can reach heights of up to 6 meters.

It is also home to a wide variety of breeding bird species, including the Grey Phalarope, the Common Shag, the Glaucous Gull and the Black Guillemot. Other species of animals that can easily be spotted here include the Common and the Grey Seals who regularly sunbathe on the many islands.

- **Deildartunguhver**

The strongest hot spring in Europe is Deildartunguhver, where the waters reach temperatures of 100°. The water is used to warm houses in various towns and villages in the area. The pipes from Deildartunguhver to Akranes are 64 kilometers long, and has an average temperature of 80° once it reaches its intended destinations. So this means that if you take a bath or shower in the region, the water has come from Deildartunguhver.

- **Eiríksstaðir**

If there is one historic site to visit in West Iceland, make sure its Eiríksstaðir. Known as the home of Leif the Lucky, Eiríksstaðir is the place where kids and adults alike can really get to know the Viking era on the Red Farm – the birthplace of this enigmatic Viking who was said to be the first European to find North America. Today, visitors can learn more about the craftsmanship skills of the past with a series of demonstrations and workshops.

- **Glymur**

The tallest waterfall in the country is Glymur. Situated in Botnsdalur Valley but be warned – the hike up is exceptionally challenging, even for those experienced hikers. You are likely to take around three or four hours hiking to get there and shouldn't really be attempted during the winter months.

- **Hallmundarhraun**

In 930, a volcanic eruption caused lava to settle right next to the Langjokull Glacier. Known as Hallmundarhraun, it consists of the lava park and the three lava caves called Surtshellir. Combined, they run for 3,500 meters, making them the longest of their kind in the country and the third, Vidgelmir, is the largest lava cave.

- **Hraunfossar**

While the lava caves they are pretty spectacular, nothing is more impressive than several waterfalls in one place. Hraunfossar is a collection of waterfalls, which flow from a subterranean river from the Hallmundarhraun, flowing into the River Hvita.

- **Kirkjufell**

Standing at an impressive 463 meters above sea level, Kirkjufell is a stunning mountain that has often featured in a variety of big-named magazines across the globe. Meaning Church Mountain in Icelandic, it resembles a tower on a church and makes for the perfect photo-shoot.

- **Snæfellsjökull,**

Snæfellsjökull sits at an altitude of 1,446 meters above sea level and is an active volcanic glacier. Over 800,000 years, the glacier has been formed to countless eruptions and is now believed to be one of several key energy centers of the world. Jules Verne used Snæfellsjökull glacier in his epic novel, *Journey to the Centre of the Earth*, published in 1864. The glacier is part of the Snæfellsjökull National Park, which was founded in 2001. Its key objectives are to safeguard the natural landscape, the historical attractions and the native flora and fauna.

- **The Library of Water**

Also known as Vatnasafn, the Library of Water was established by Roni Horn within the old library at Stykkishólmur, a town located along the coastline. The Library of Water consists of three collections of water, words and weather reports, which mirror Roni Horn's relationship with the landscape and culture of the country.

The Library of Water overlooks both the sea and the residential houses of the town. In the Water section of the library, there are 24 glass columns, which hold water from the ice taken from Icelandic glaciers. The water within the columns then reflects light onto the floor, which illuminate Icelandic and English words connected to the weather.

Top Attractions for Kids

For kids, West Iceland is a great place to explore and learn. There are some fantastic family-friendly restaurants and accommodations, and plenty of attractions to captivate kids of all ages.

- **Swimming Pools**

West Iceland has an abundance of swimming pools to enjoy of all sizes. As they are all heated, you can be sure you won't freeze in these waters. The majority are located outdoors but there are several which are indoors. Don't be surprised to share the pools with locals at every time of the year.

- **Bjarteyjasandur**

Situated within Hvalfjordur, Bjarteyjasandur is a working farm open to the public. Kids came come here to see and interact with sheep, horses, chickens, dogs, cars and rabbits bred for their wool. The rural life of the West Icelanders is exceptionally rich and interesting, and kids can run about as they learn. During the winter, visitors are advised to ring the farm to make sure they are taking visitors that day.

- **Bjössaróló**

There will be times when kids just need to let loose some energy and run around. There's no better place to do this than at Bjössaróló. The playground was constructed in the late 1970s by Bjorn H Gudmundsson from Borgarnes using scrap materials. Today, it's a fantastically small theme park guaranteed to delight – and wear out the kids!

- **Caving**

Mostly for older kids, there are two caves where kids – and adults – can go caving with guides. Vatnshellir is 8,000 years old and can be found within Snæfellsjökull National Park; guides can only be hired during the winter but the caves are open throughout the year. The other cave to visit is the previously mentioned Viðgelmir, the biggest lava cave in the country and be found in Borgarfjörður, but kids need to be at least eight years old to enter.

- **Erpsstaðir**

Erpstaðir is another working farm visitors can visit, with a variety of animals to see and pet. They also sell a range of fresh foods to try including cheeses, ice cream and chocolates. In the winter, it is advisable to book in advance.

- **Garðarlundur Park**

Garðalundur Park is located with Akranes, highly popular with locals and tourists alike. This is where most people will come for all occasions; so don't be surprised if you see parties or big gatherings here. Several ponds can be found scattered throughout the park, providing homes and sustenance for various bird species.

- **Háafell**

Haafell is often referred to as the Goat Centre of the country and is the birthplace of the Icelandic goats. Indeed, it is one of the few places in the country that breeds these particular species of goat and the best place to interact with them. Kids and adults can stroke the goats and then purchase a range of goat-related products, including cheese and soap. Just be sure to ring and make sure they are open during the winter months.

- **Horse-Riding**

For horse lovers, there are several places in West Iceland where you can hire a horse and explore the surrounding region with these magnificent creatures. Obviously, inform the stables that there will be kids with you so they pick the right, safer horses for your little ones.

- **The Settlement Centre**

For kids with a passion for history, there is no better place than the Settlement Centre. Here, kids will learn more about the Settlement of Iceland and about the famous Viking, Egill Skallagrimsson, as well as the rest of Icelandic history and culture.

- **Fossatún Troll Park**

Iceland boasts a rich legacy of mythological creatures and beings, with trolls being just one of them. At the Fossatun Troll Park, kids can play a variety of troll-related games including golf, and count how many troll statues they can find throughout the park.

Nightlife in West Iceland

Unfortunately, if you're searching for a pulsating nightlife, full of loud music and numerous clubs, you are not going to find it in West Iceland. This is an area of calmness and serenity, but there are several pubs you can enjoy.

- **RuBen**

Located in Grundarfjorour, RuBen is a pub and restaurant. The menu is simple and the beers cheap and enjoyable. Down a few drinks in a comfortable setting whilst enjoying a variety of delicious dishes.

- **Sjavarpakkhusid**

Sjavarpakkhusid is another pub restaurant located in Stykkisholmur, which is popular with locals and visitors alike due to their Happy Hour. The menu offers a range of tasty foods and the bar is stacked with a good supply of beers, wines and spirits.

Chapter 4: Westfjords Iceland

The northwest region of Iceland known as the Westfjords is one of the country's well-preserved destination. Westfjords have unspoiled wilderness primarily due to the regions isolated location. It is largely uninhabited, which is one of the reasons why it is a must-see destination for serious explorers.

An uninhabited peninsula called Hornstrandir is located in the northwest corner of the Westfjords. It is also a nature reserve that houses a variety of bird life and the Arctic fox. The Látrabjarg bird cliff located on Westfjords' west side hosts almost half of some bird species of the world. It is also Europe's westernmost point. The Dynjandi is a spectacular set of waterfalls, which is about 100 meters in height. It is also a must-see for travelers and visitors of the Westfjords.

The region's culture is primarily brought about by heritage and tradition. Westfjords cuisine and folklore speak a lot about the region's strong relation with the ocean. There are also museums that focus on creatures and monsters from the sea and witchcraft and sorcery.

Westfjords region is an authentic Icelandic wilderness, which is ideal for spotting and watching unique fauna, birds, and arctic fox in their natural habitats.

Transportation

Although the region of Westfjords is a remote part of Iceland, it is accessible via various kinds of transport system.

For instance, travelers and visitors can get to the Westfjords by air by taking a flight from Iceland's capital Reykjavík to the chosen destination. It would take about 40 to 50 minutes to get to the Westfjords via plane.

Travelers and visitors can also rent and drive a car to go from one destination to another in the Westfjords. From Reykjavík to Ísafjörður, it would take a 455-kilometer ride on paved road. From Reykjavík to Þingeyri, it would take a 408-kilometer ride, 271 kilometers of which is on paved road.

The Westfjords are also accessible via bus tours. Bus schedules are available all throughout the year in several routes, including Reykjavík – Hólmavík; Hólmavík – Ísafjörður; and Reykjavík – Brjánslækur via ferry Baldur. For inquiries on these routes, travelers may visit www.bus.is. The route from Brjánslækur – Patreksfjörður is also available all year round. For inquiries on this route, traveler may visit www.wa.is.

The Baldur, which is a car ferry, also operates in the Westfjords. It operates between Stykkishólmur and Brjánslækur with two departures from June to August. The departure from Stykkishólmur is daily during the winter months.

Where to Go in the Westfjords

- ## *Natural History Museum of Bolungarvík*

Located in the Bolungarvík center, the museum boasts of an exhibition of a variety of natural items, including stuffed sea and land mammals and more than 250 stuffed birds from breeder in Iceland. The museum also features a collection of rocks and minerals from Steinn Emilsson, a local geologist. It also exhibits old lignite testimonial pieces for the ancient forest of Iceland from some million years ago.

The museum also displays the jaw, which belonged to the largest blue whale caught in Iceland. The display that also includes a set of posters about Icelandic whales and whaling is a project between the museum and the botanical garden in Dýrafjörður called Skrúður.

The Natural History Museum of Bolungarvík has a new display about ravens, which include a real nest, artifacts, and stories, which depict the relationship of the bird specie with the culture of Iceland over the years.

During weekdays from June 1 to August 16, the museum open from 9 in the morning to 5 in the afternoon and 10 in the morning to 5 in the afternoon during weekends. In winter, the museum opens from 9 in the morning to 5 in the afternoon during weekdays only.

- ## *The Arctic Fox Center*

A non-profit research and exhibition center, the Arctic Fox Center primarily revolves on the *Vulpes lagopus* or the arctic fox, which is Iceland's only native mundane mammal. On September 15, 2007, 42 founders, including local people, municipalities, and tourist operators in the Westfjords, established the center in Sudavik Westfjords. All founders share a common interest in the native terrestrial mammal with the belief that it could increase Iceland's ecotourism. Professor Pall Hersteinsson of the University of Iceland conceptualized the Arctic Fox Center with the objective of collecting every available material and knowledge pertinent to the arctic fox in the present and the past.

The Arctic Fox Center is home to an exhibition that educates travelers and visitors about various information about the arctic fox. These include the history and biology of the arctic fox as a species; the struggle between people and the arctic fox since the early Icelandic settlement; the specialties and status of the arctic fox in Iceland; fox hunting as Iceland's oldest paid operation, stories, materials, and descriptions; and fox farming activities for the wild population.

The Arctic Fox Center is open from 10 in the morning to 2 in the afternoon in October until April from 9 in the morning to the evening in May until September.

- ***Memorial Museum Kört***

The Memorial Museum Kört is located in Trékyllisvík creek in Strandir. It boasts of a display of local arts, crafts, and old artifacts from the area. It used to be a house made out of driftwood. It is surrounded by sea, mountains, a rocky cost, seals, and birds. Its owner, Valgeir Benediktsson who built the house has a collection of old things from the area. Benediktsson is an artists and usually makes use of driftwood and other types of wood in Iceland in his artwork. Local people, travelers, and visitors can purchase his works in Kört.

Guided tours are also provided in the Memorial Museum Kört. Light refreshments and coffee are available in the museum.

From June 1 to August 31, the museum opens from 10 in the morning to 6 in the evening. From September 1 to May 31, the museum opens only upon prior booking or agreement.

- ### *Ósvör Maritime Museum*

This museum is a replica of a 19th century Icelandic fishing station. The Ósvör Maritime Museum displays a crew hut with tools, a rowing boat, a drying shed, and a salt house. The curator of the museum is dressed in a traditional fisherman outfit as he welcomes guests.

The museum opens from 9 in the morning to 5 in the afternoon during weekdays and 10 in the morning to 5 in the afternoon during weekends for the months of June until August. On the other hand, the museum only opens during winter through a prior appointment.

- ### Látrabjarg

Látrabjarg ranks as one of the most awe-inspiring sights in the Westfjords region. This cliff is home to countless birds and is the westernmost point in the entire country. It's actually made up of several cliffs over 14 kilometers long and stretches up to a height of 441 meters. Be careful when hiking up to the top as the climb is quite steep. As the birds are safe from predators, they are unafraid and provide the perfect photo-shoot, even close up shots. Be careful as you edge your way closer to the cliffs trying to see the puffins, as some of the rocks are loose. However, Látrabjarg makes for a stunning experience.

- **Hornbjarg**

Hornbjarg is another mesmerising cliff in the Westfjords area, home to a great colony of seafowl. The tallest areas stand up to 543 meters above sea level and were once known as the Western Horn. It is also associated with the ancient Sagas, making it a rich cultural attraction as well as a magnificent scenic area. Hornvik is a fishing hamlet and can be found on the cove, and boasts a long history of its own. In years past, this was a popular area to catch sea birds and collecting eggs.

- **Dynjandi**

Dynjandi is undoubtedly the most breath-taking place within Westfjords. For years, it has been a popular scene to plaster all over magazines, travel related or not. Dynjandi is a waterfall, with the wider section being the favorite for photographers to shoot. Yet, as you travel down the river, you will come across equally as stunning, albeit smaller, waterfalls to enjoy. There is even one that visitors can walk along if they have the nerve to do so!

- **Svalvogar**

Svalvogar is a nearly 50-kilometer-long circuit between Dýrafjörður and Arnarfjörður which follows the tapered coast line around the bluff – please note, this should not be done when the tides come in – and then returns via the Kaldbakur route, bypassing the highest mountains in the Westfjords mountain range. Svalvogar is often referred to as the Dream Road, and with its captivating scenery of dramatic coastline, endless mountains and azure-drenched skies, it's not hard to see why.

- **Natural Hot Springs**

Throughout the Westfjords region, there are numerous natural hot springs to be found, even in the most isolated parts. The locations of some of these springs won't be found in a guide book – they are guarded by locals or just discovered by visitors as they are exploring the area. The Westfjords area is often speculated to be a geological hot spot and isn't as noticeable as other parts of Iceland. So when you come across one of these springs, enjoy the warm waters, which are fed from underground. Some can be found along the coastline, allowing you soak your aching muscles whilst enjoying stunning views across the ocean.

- **Sculptures in Selardalur**

Within Selardalur Valley in Arnarfjordur, the sculptures and buildings of Samuel Jonsson were restored by a local foundation. With the help of a sculptor from Germany, international volunteers and locals, they have begun to work on construction of an inn for artists and writers, as well as a museum dedicated to art and the sculptures.

- **Valagil**

If you are searching for outstanding beauty, look no further than Valagil. This amazing gorge boasts a fast-flowing waterfall that was created from multiple layers of lava. Valagil is situated close to Álftafjörður, near Súðavík, and all you need to do to reach it is to follow the footpath well mapped out from the road. According to locals, the gorge takes its name from the falcons that used to make their homes here, although others claim it was named in honor of a lady named Vala who, centuries ago fell from it and died.

- **Reykjarfjordur by Fjord Arnarfjordur**

Located in Reykjarfjodur, this massive outdoor swimming pool is heated by natural hot waters from underground, and is open all year round for visitors to enjoy. Once you've finished at the pool, head upwards and discover a charming natural hot spring to try out. Best of all, they're both free!

- **Vigur**

From Ísafjörður, take a boat to Vigur where you can immerse yourself in stunning natural beauty. This island features an abundance of bird species, including puffins and arctic terns. The majority of the island has been dug out by the puffins, who create their nests here, so visitors are highly recommended to stick to the path created in order to avoid falling into one! This iconic bird is often referred to as the northern penguin, and they create a wonderful scene to photograph. The arctic terns are just as beautiful but they are incredibly territorial. Visitors are recommended to hold onto a stick or something, which they can hold into the air should they start seeing you as a threat. You may even see locals come here to feed the chicks of the eider colony, who allow the humans to collect their down. The town itself is steeped in charm, boasting the smallest post office in the country, the only windmill in Iceland and a collection of lovely homes.

- **Patreksfjörður**

In the southern part of the Westfjords lies the largest town – Patreksfjörður. Boasting a population of around 660 people, the town used to be the forefront of the country's fishing industry and was the first to establish trawler fishing. Fishing is still today's biggest industry, as well as fish farms and other related businesses. However, if fish aren't your thing, then the town also holds a number of other attractions to enjoy.

The town is easily reachable from Latrabjarg Cliffs, Dynjandi Waterfall and Raudasandur beach. There's a great outdoor swimming pool to enjoy, or several natural hot water springs scattered just outside the town if you fancy them. Hotels and guesthouses are aplenty in town, along with tour guides who can show you around the region.

For visitors who enjoy the more cultural side of things, the town boasts two museums not to be missed out on – the Hnjotur Folk Museum and the Pirate Museum. Explore the history and culture of the local area through a range of well laid-out exhibitions and displays, including those on egg picking along the cliff-face, which was perilous for gatherers. The pirate museum boasts some wonderful boats and other objects. If you head to Hnjotur you should pay a visit to the

Aviation Museum where you can immerse yourself in Iceland's history of flying.

If you head towards the coast of Patreksfjörður then you should pay a visit to the pirate workshop. Perfect for families, the modern-day pirates take you on a fascinating journey on pirate life, helping visitors learn about how to navigate on the waters and what they used to wear. Pirates-in-training can even have their meals at the long tables pirates themselves would have used to eat at! Ha ha me hearties, it's a pirate's life for sure!

Nightlife in Westfjords

The majority of nightclubs and swanky bars can be found at the capital; in Westfjords, nightlife is much more relaxed. Relax in one of the numerous pubs sipping on a drink, or two, whilst watching the football on the widescreen television.

- ***Edda Hotel Isafjordur***

The Edda Hotel Isafjordur is Isafjordur's only pub and hotel, which is housed in a former school. Quite basic, but the food and drink is good, reasonable priced, and has wi-fi.

Where to Stay in the Westfjords

- ## *Hotel Laugarholl*

For most Icelanders, the Westfjords are full of mystery, especially in the Strandir area. This is due to folklore that Strandir is home to both good and evil witchcraft, elves, ghosts, and even trolls.

Hotel Laugarholl is situated in the remote wilderness of Strandir. It is a peaceful family-run country hotel in the sparsely inhabited Bjarnarfjordur valley. It offers private and shared facilities, a restaurant that caters homemade local food and global cuisine, and a cozy living room with free WiFi access. The rooms are available in single, double, and family rooms.
One of the highlights of Hotel Laugarholl is its proximity to the Pool of Gvendur, which is a geothermal outdoor swimming pool with warm water of 32 degrees and an adjacent natural pool with water of 42 degrees. Hotel guests can have a warm dip in the pools after a long day of hiking or road tripping.

Hotel Laugarholl is 258 kilometers from Reykjavík; 250 kilometers from Isafjordur; 190 kilometers from Stykkishólmur; and 360 kilometers from Akureyri.

For booking and other information, travelers and visitors may visit their website www.laugarholl.is

- ## *Fisherman Hotel*

Fisherman Hotel is a popular hotel in the Sudureyri area. It is equipped with up-to-date accommodation. It offers single, double, and family rooms, either with or without private accommodation. Each room has a telephone, washbasin, and hair dryer. The hotel also has a self-catering facility and offers free WiFi connection. The entire establishment is a non-smoking environment. The hotel also offers free pickup service from the airport of Isafjordur.

Guests of the Fisherman Hotel have the chance to learn how the local people practice a sustainable and eco-friendly village. Guests can also try the hotel's sumptuous seafood menu with an authentic Westfjords cooking style.

The Fisherman Hotel offers a seafood trail tour where guests can participate in a culinary and cultural experience. The tour includes listening to local storytellers, leaning about how the Sudureyri is called "heaven on earth," catching the finest fish in Iceland, and tasting the freshest fish at the Kitchen restaurant.

For booking information and prices, travelers and visitors may visit www.fisherman.is

- ***Hotel Flatey***

Located in the center of Flatey's old village in Breiðafjörður, Hotel Flatey offers 7 twin or double rooms, suites, 1 family room for 3 persons, and 2 single rooms. It was formerly timber houses dating from the times of prosperity of the island. Most of the houses have already been restored.

Hotel Flatey has guest rooms and a dining room situated in converted warehouses in the old market square. Hotel guests can enjoy the unique atmosphere of the island. During the stay of guests, they can try the choice food offered while relishing the view of the nesting grounds of the Arctic terns, the coastline, and the village.

Chapter 5: Reykjanes Peninsula

Iceland's geothermal wonder is the Reykjanes peninsula, which is a popular destination for travelers and tourists. It is where lighthouses are greater in number than the villages. It is also where the Keflavík International Airport is located.

The Reykjanes peninsula is near the Blue Lagoon. It is home to a number of high-temperature geothermal areas. Three of the geothermal areas generate electricity. In addition, travelers and visitors get to see clearly the junction in the crust of the Earth between the American and European tectonic plates in the Reykjanes peninsula.

This part of Iceland boasts of unique recreational activities as well as various tourist destinations in its rugged landscape. The Reykjanes peninsula features caves, volcanic craters, geothermal waters, lava fields, and hot springs. It also has a wide range of restaurants, churches, museums, festivals, and lighthouses.

Transportation

The Reykjanes Peninsula is said to be the gateway to Iceland. Travelers and visitors can get to the area via plane, car ferry, cruise ship, or car.

More often than not, travelers arrive in Iceland at the Keflavik International Airport, which is 50 kilometers west of the capital Reykjavík and northwest of the Reykjanes peninsula. There are two main air carriers available, including Iceland Air and Wow Air, both of which fly all over Europe and the United States.

There are also travelers who opt to get to Reykjanes peninsula via the Smyril Line car ferry, which travels from Europe via the Faroe Islands and docks at the Seyðisfjörður located in the east coast of Iceland. From there, travelers can drive to Reykjanes peninsula in about 8 – 9 hours. There are also cruise ships that dock daily at the Reykjavík Harbor, especially during summer.

Travelers and visitors who like to explore various places in Iceland can drive from Reykjavík through the Hafnafjörður village, taking road 41, which is a highway along the north shore going to the Keflavik International Airport. Those who come from South Iceland, Hveragerði, or Selfoss can drive southwest to Thorlakshöfn, taking road 425 and 427 along the peninsula's south coast via Grindavik, going round the peninsula's perimeter, and back to Reykjavík.

Where to Go in the Reykjanes Peninsula

- ## *The Blue Lagoon*

Tourists who want to experience healthy, geothermal spa can head to the Blue Lagoon in the Reykjanes peninsula. This is a place where travelers and visitors are able to become one with nature, breathe fresh and clean air, and enjoy the beautiful scene while soaking up in the relaxing geothermal seawater.

Blue Lagoon was voted as the world's best spa and one of National Geographic's 25 wonders of the world. It has been awarded the Blue Flag environmental recognition for 10 consecutive years. This award is given to natural marinas and beaches.

Having six million liters of geothermal seawater, the water temperature in Blue Lagoon ranges from 37 degrees to 39 degrees. Based on regular sampling, "common" bacteria cannot grow in this ecosystem; thus, it does not chlorine or other additional cleansers.

Apart from the lagoon, a psoriasis clinic is also found in the area. The Blue Lagoon psoriasis clinic provides natural geothermal treatment for psoriasis with the aid of the Icelandic Health Authorities. The Icelandic Social Insurance pays for the treatment cost of Icelandic psoriasis patients. The clinic has a modern look and features practical solutions. There is a designated area in the lagoon to meet the needs of the Clinic. For instance, the lagoon area has a 350-square meter of outdoor lagoon and a 50-square meter indoor pool.

Blue Lagoon also offers accommodation with 35 double rooms. Each room is spacious and well designed with a porch, television, Internet access, and a private bathroom. Blue Lagoon also has a living area, dining room, and a fitness area with weight lifting stations and cardiovascular equipment.

- ***Reykjanes***

Reykjanes is located in the southwest end of the peninsula. It is where travelers and visitors can find the Mid-Atlantic Ridge, rising out of the sea. Reykjanes is a part of Iceland's largest urban area, Suðurnes. Most travelers go to this area as they enter or leave Iceland.

Reykjanes offers a magnificent presentation of nature. It has several volcanic formations as well as hills and mountains made of volcanic stuff. It also features distinct types of volcanic edifices and volcanoes, and small and large lava flows.

Reykjanes has a number of marine birds, which are common in the peninsula. Most travelers and visitors become easily attracted by the different species of birds, especially during breeding season. There are also Arctic terns and gulls in Reykjanes, which are seen via high sea cliffs

The main activities in Reykjanes include fishing and agriculture. Local people are skilled in cultivation revolving around reforestation, vegetation, reclamation of soils, and gardening.

Reykjanes offers tourist services that take travelers to various places and outdoor activities.

- *Eldey*

Eldey is a high rock of about 77 meters high, which protrudes out of the sea. It is located 15 kilometers to the southwestern tip of the Reykjanes peninsula. Its structure is made of basaltic hyaloclastites.

Eldey is the innermost or deepest area of a skerries chain, which stands on a submarine ridge, stretching 45 sea miles offshore to the southwestern coast. The chain of skerries is known as the Eldeyjar or Fuglasker. Geirfuglasker was one of the skerries in which the Great Auk's last colony breeding was located. However, it disappeared from the surface in 1830 during submarine eruptions.

It is believed that Eldey still has one of the largest gannet colonies. In 1949, the number of gannets breeding in Eldey was 70,000, specifically during summer.

- *Keilir*

The most distinctive Reykjanes landmark is a hyaloclastite mountain known as Keilir. It is also said to be the peninsula's symbol. During the ice age, Keilir was created through subglacial eruptions. Geologists claim that it has a crater plug and its shape is the factor, which makes it distinctive. The climb to Keilir is not as difficult as it may look although its slopes are steep. Adventurers who climb the mountain will surely have an unforgettable experience as the view from its top s magnificent. The mountaintop is like a concrete table that has a view direction map on a plate.

Travelers and visitors can drive using 4x4 cars on Höskuldarvegi. Parking is available at Oddafell. From the parking, a trail of about 3 kilometers is available to reach Keilir.

- **Reykjanesviti Lighthouse**

Reykjanesviti lighthouse is the oldest of its kind in Iceland. But not only is it a striking and famous historical building around the world, but it is set in an equally impressive location. There were actually two lighthouses bearing the same name; the first was constructed in 1878 but an earthquake caused serious damage nine years later. The second version, the one you see today, was constructed in 1907 and is set upon Baejarfell Hill. Not only are the views from here unparalleled, but also the geothermal fields located at the base of Baejarfell Hill send wafts of steam upwards, creating a stunning atmosphere to it.

- **Gunnuhver Geothermal Area**

The geothermal mud pools located at Gunnuhver are spread over the southwest region of the Reykjanes Peninsular. They are named after a woman who over four centuries ago when she fell into them. The biggest natural hot spring is more than 20 meters wide and sits within an edge of mud as steam ascends to the skies. They can be found not far from the Reykjanesviti Lighthouse and the Bridge Between Continents and provide the perfect location to experience the dramatic Icelandic landscape. Stay on the bridge and look down to watch the bubbling of the hot waters.

- **The Bridge Between Continents**

Iceland is drifting away from the Mid-Atlantic Ridge at around two centimeters each year. Head up to the top of Reykjanes Peninsular where you actually see the boundaries between North America and Europe. Get in the right position and you can have each foot in complete different continents! Once you have finished the short circuit across the bridge, you will receive a certificate stating your achievement – this can be attained at the tourist information office and can be found around seven kilometers from Hafnir.

- **Brimketill Lava Rock Pool**

Head down the coast to Grindavik and you will stumble across the Brimketill Lava Rock Pool. The volcanic waters are safe enough to swim in, although some visitors may find the plunge a little too hair-raising! According to stories, a woman with the appearance of a troll, who was named Oddny, used to live here, although today no one has seen anyone who fits her description.

- **Vikingworld Iceland**

You can't expect to visit Iceland and not visit Vikingworld Iceland! Located in Reykjanesbaer, this award-winning museum features a variety of highly interesting and interactive exhibitions for visitors to enjoy and learn, as well as boasting a petting zoo in the summer months, a children's playground and a classroom for visitors to hear talks about the Vikings. The highlight of Vikingworld Iceland is a genuine Viking ship that was constructed by Gunnae Marel Eggertsson back in the mid-1990s. In 2000, it completed a successful expedition from Iceland to New York. If you are interested in learning more about Iceland's Viking heritage, then Vikingworld Iceland is certainly the place to go.

- **The Saltfisksetrið Exhibition**

Grindavik boasts a long, rich seafaring history, there's no better place to explore this legacy than at the Saltfisksetrið exhibition. The cod industry has long been an important part of local economy, and this is highlighted at the museum, using well-planned displays of interesting objects. While here, head over to the Salt fish Museum in order to learn more about local history and culture.

- **Kirkjuvogsbás Beach**

The waters of the North Atlantic Ocean are cold; the waters from a geothermal power plant are hot. When the two combine, you get something incredible at Kirkjuvogsbas Beach. The beach is located around twenty minutes away from Keflavik Airport and has long been a top destination in the entire country for tourists wanting to brave the waters and enjoy outstanding views across the waters.

- **The Grindavík Harbor**

Located within Grindavik Town, the harbor has long been the heart and soul, not just of the local community, but of the town's fishing industry. Each day, numerous boats sail in and out of the harbor. Relax, sit back and watch the boats go sailing past as you enjoy a hot drink from the cafes located along the harbor-front.

Nightlife in Reykjanes Peninsula

There are a number of good quality pubs to enjoy in this region, although don't expect any heart-pumping nightclubs to dance the night away.

- **Bryggjan**

Located along the shorefront in Grindavik, Bryggjan offers a nice, cost setting in which to enjoy a variety of meals and a good selection of beers, wines and spirits. It also boasts free Wi-Fi, great service and the chance to interact with some of the locals who frequent the pub.

- **Fish House Bar and Grill**

A bar and restaurant combined, visitors can enjoy a few drinks in an energetic, vibrant setting in Grindavik town. Simple food, great drinks, friendly atmosphere ... what more could you need?

- **Paddy's Irish Pub**

Located in Keflavik, Paddy's Irish Bar is fun, friendly and full of your favorite tipple! It takes around ten minutes to get to from the town's hotel area, it enjoys a cozy atmosphere and friendly customers who like to socialize.

Where to Eat in the Reykjanes Peninsula

- ## *Lava Restaurant*

Lava Restaurant is located in the premises of Blue Lagoon. It is built in the cliff, which provides a natural lava wall as well as a good view of the lagoon. Guests will surely have a unique experience in this restaurant when it comes to dining.

The house chef boasts of the restaurant's menu using Icelandic ingredients, creating light dishes and gourmet meals. The freshest available fish visitors can find is during the day as local people in the fishing village of Grindavík sell their catch.

- ## *Salthúsið Restaurant*

Salthúsið Restaurant is a cozy log house, which offers authentic Icelandic cuisine. It is also known as the House of Bacalao or codfish, which was an important factor in the economy of Iceland specifically on the Icelandic Coat of Arms. Located in Grindavik, Salthúsið Restaurant is the first in the entire country to specialize in codfish.

- ## *Hja Höllu*

Located in Grindavik, Hja Höllu is a restaurant that offers sumptuous, fresh, healthy, and nutrient-filled food as well as simple drinks. Its menu includes fresh local fish, chicken, sandwiches, salad, soup, wraps, pizza, and vegetarian dishes.

The restaurant's dishes are prepared and cooked from natural ingredients. Its cooler features juices and yogurt. Freshly made cakes and bread are also available. Mos guests order Hja Höllu's daily bag, which includes food good for one entire day. Thus, travelers and visitors can opt for this bag and enjoy Iceland without stopping to grab something to eat. The daily bag includes lunch, boost, fresh juices, snacks, and dessert.

Hja Höllu is open daily from 8 in the morning. During weekends, it opens from 10 in the morning.

Where to Stay in the Reykjanes Peninsula

- ## *Hotel Keflavik*

Hotel Keflavik was established in 1986 and has been a popular accommodation in Iceland. It is only 5 minutes away from the Keflavik International Airport, 40 minutes away from Iceland's capital, Reykjavík, and just 15 minutes away from Blue Lagoon. The hotel features newly renovated rooms, a fully equipped fitness area with step aerobics and spinning classes, a solarium, an elegant restaurant, and a relaxing sauna.

Hotel Keflavik is a family-run hotel. It is first class with 4-star accommodations. The hotel provides rental cars, transportation services, concierge services, and free parking to its guests. It also features an on-site fitness center and complimentary breakfast.

For prices and booking information, visit their website www.kef.is.

- ## *Diamond Suites*

Diamond Suites is a five star boutique hotel situated on the top floor of the renowned Hotel Keflavik. It features suites, which are decorated individually with a distinct style and character. It also features a library suite made of wood, a spa suite, and a unique suite with walls made of white leather. Guests will surely fine the hotel cozy whether they are inclined to modern design or old-world charm. Each suite provides an atmosphere that guests prefer. In addition, the luxury furniture is handpicked so guests can truly enjoy their stay.

Diamond Suites hotel is home to the famous KEF Restaurant. This restaurant is popular among travelers of Europe and Alaska. Its specialty is Jenny Runarsdottir's fish cod. KEF Restaurant is situated under a glass facade on the hotel's ground floor. Guests can also request a private chef to prepare dinner in their room or in the restaurant. Truly, Diamond Suites hotel offers personal service, luxury, and a unique experience to its guests.

For prices and booking information, interested parties may visit their website www.diamondsuites.is

- ***Hotel Vogar***

Hotel Vogar is located near the Keflavik International Airport and just a few minutes drive to Blue Lagoon and Iceland's capital, Reykjavík. It is a perfect accommodation for visitors going in and out of Iceland.

Hotel Vogar features 2 family apartments and 37 rooms with WiFi access and satellite television. It also offers a sumptuous breakfast buffet.

For interested parties, visit www.hotelvogar.is

What to Do in the Reykjanes Peninsula

There are various activities travelers and visitors can do in the peninsula of Reykjanes. They can experience North Island in small groups or privately through qualified guides who are adept in the lands ins and outs. Travelers and visitors will surely enjoy their adventure in the peninsula, which is filled with sights, destinations, and interactive activities that they will never find in other places.

One of the most prominent year-round operators is the Saga travel, which operates during summer and even winter. It offers package tours, pre-organized day tours, excursions and sightseeing from different destinations, including Lake Myvatn, Reykjavík, and Akureyri to the most extraordinary places in the Reykjanes peninsula.

Some of the tours include local food and gourmet, Lake Myvatn excursion, Askja Super Jeep tour, Waterfall Dettifos – Super Jeep tour, Cave Exploration – Lofthellir, Farmers Passion, Countryside Culture, Northern Lights, Whales and Waterfalls tour, hiking tours, bike tours, horseback riding, and Deep Sea angling.

Multi-day tours are also available for travelers and adventurers with different lifestyles. These tours include slow travel, night travel, bird watching, and geology.

Super Jeeps and private guiding are popular among tourists. These are usually arranged from an hour to a multi-day tour during weekdays or weekends, day or night, and in any season.

Private tours are also available, which include whale watching, flora, eruptions and volcano's history, geology, mythology of trolls and elves, folk and fairy tales, and photography among others.

More often than not, the tour services offered in the peninsula of Reykjanes are tailor-made to fit the preferences of travelers and visitors.

Chapter 6: Reykjavik – Little Capital of Iceland

Reykjavík is known as the little capital of Iceland as its population is just 120,000. There are only a few skyscrapers in the city as compared to other capitals of other countries. Traffic is also rare and local people usually know each other. Reykjavík features activities and events that keep it pulsing and alive with cheer and joy.

More often than not, it is sunny in this part of Iceland. As such, picnickers and sunbathers fill the Austurvöllur, the green square situated in front of the Parliament. Tourists and local people also stroll down the Laugavegur, which is the center of shopping and dining. When happy hours come, tourists can enjoy outdoor seating provided in bars for some enjoyment and people watching. Entertainers usually line the sidewalks of Reykjavík while performance artists take the stage to present their surprise acts. In fact, anything can happen in Reykjavík, including a marching band that appears randomly.

In 101 or the downtown Reykjavík, travelers and visitors can enjoy the arts scene and rich culture of Iceland. During the day, the downtown is primarily a café-culture. Most of the cafes provide free Internet access to their guests and even refills their coffees. More often than not, guests tend to linger in the cafes for hours, keeping the city lively with their conversations. During the night, on the other hand, people tend to go to the excellent restaurants in the city.

Playful street art and playful murals are found all throughout the 101. These attest the sense of fun and creativity of Reykjavík. There are also art galleries in the city, including the National Gallery and the Reykjavík Art Museum, which exhibits the works of prominent Icelandic artists. In addition, small independent galleries showcase the contemporary projects of both international and Icelandic artists.

Most of the museums in Reykjavík is committed to preserve the country's history and culture. Reykjavík has been designated as a UNESCO City of Literature. It is also the center of the country's literary heritage in which travelers and visitors can discover a wealth of literary work and a treasure of skilled authors and poets.

One of the keystones of the cultural life in Reykjavík is local music. There are various musical acts that describe a wide range of musical genres, including bluegrass folk, rap lo-fi, reggae, punk rock, and even death metal.

Icelandic musicians are usually featured in downtown record stores although tourists can easily experience acts live in street concerts. Most clubs and bars also host live shows regularly, drawing huge crowds of both friends and fans. Travelers and visitors in Reykjavík usually cap their hectic day by catching live music on the town.

Reykjavík is famous for its animated nightlife, which starts late and ends early in the morning. Most clubs are filled around midnight as the party starts until the morning. For local people, familiar faces are not difficult to find during a night out.

Reykjavík is often the starting point of travelers and visitors when touring Iceland. Apart from being the capital of the country, it features rich natural beauty, history, and culture. For instance, Reykjavík offers various day trips from the city to the nearby hot springs, mountains, volcanoes, and glaciers. Most day excursions include glacier climbing, caving, horseback riding, whale watching, and river rafting among others.

In downtown Reykjavík, galleries, museums, cafes, theaters, and swimming pools keep tourists busy. The restaurants in downtown Reykjavík often serve seafood, lamb, and other exotic delicacies.

Many find Reykjavík as a city of contrasts given that it is a small town and at the same time cosmopolitan. It is full of history although it is young at heart. It is sophisticated during the day and vibrant during the night. There are a number of monuments, both old and new. Harpa is one of the newly built music and conference centers, which is located in front of the ocean.

The best way to explore Reykjavík, as it is only a small town, is by bike or foot.

Where to Go in Reykjavík

- *Krýsuvík Geothermal Area*

Krýsuvík geothermal area is a place where travelers and visitors find remarkable solfatara fields near the Hafnafjörður center. Krýsuvík has a surface area that features boiling hot springs, and volcanic vents, which are surrounded by several colorful hills. There is a winding boardwalk through the rippling and bubbling geothermal area. The boardwalk is well maintained and equipped with instructive as well as informative signage about pertinent geological facts. The large massive solfatara is worth the walk as it is offers a spectacular view of the areas surrounding it. In addition, the solfatara steams away on the hilltop, which fires up the curiosity of tourists and local people.

Travelers and visitors can also explore the stunning Krýsuvíkurbjarg cliffs as a side-trip. The cliffs are known for its unique birdlife.

Apart from the sulphur deposits and mudpots, the Krýsuvík geothermal area also has extremely colorful crater lakes, including the Gestsstaðavatn, Grænavatn, and ad Augun lakes. These are explosion craters brought about by volcanic eruptions. The largest of the three lakes mentioned is the Grænavatn Lake, which is about 150 feet deep. It is colored given that the thermal algae and crystals in it absorb sunlight; thus, it glows in an extremely deep green. The name Gestsstaðavatn, on the other hand, comes from a nearby farm, Getsstaðir. During the middle ages, the farm was abandoned. The main road's adjacent side has Augun, which features to small lakes side by side to each other. Augun means eyes.

Not far from Krýsuvík geothermal area, travelers and visitors can drive to the Krýsuvíkurberg Cliffs, which features a stunning view. It presents thousands of sea birds nesting in the hillside and just beside the Atlantic surf. Travelers and visitors can also hike along the cliffs' edges for a peaceful experience of nature. While hiking, it is possible to see guillemots, kittiwakes, and other bird species frolicking with their flocks or diving into the sea.

A detailed map of the Krýsuvík geothermal area is provided in the Hafnarfjörður Tourist Information Center for walking and hiking routes as well as pertinent information on attractions, local history, folklore, and geology.

- ***Hallgrímskirkja Church***

The main landmark of Reykjavík is the Hallgrímskirkja church, which was designed in 1937 by Guðjón Samuel. The tower of the church is seen from almost all parts of the city. The works of Samuel, including the church, were inspired by the charming forms and shapes made when lava cools down into basalt rocks.

In 1945, the church's construction began; however, it only ended in 1986. The tower was the first to be completed before the rest of the church. In 1948, the crypt situated beneath the choir was consecrated. In 1974, the wings and steeple were completed. Finally, 1986 was the year of the consecration of the nave.

Hallgrímskirkja church is notable for its gargantuan pipe organ, which Johannes Klais, a German organ builder designed and constructed. The pipe organ has a height of 15 meters and weighs around 25 tons. It is driven by a pedal and 4 manuals, 72 stops, 102 ranks, and 5275 pipes, which are all designed to provide powerful notes that fill the church with the organ's range of tones. The pipe organ produces dulcet to dramatic tones. In December 1992, the construction of the pipe organ was completed. Since then, it is used in various recordings, including some of Christopher Herrick's compositions.

A fine statue of Leifur Eiriksson, the first European who discovered America, stands directly in the church's front. Leifur is said to have lande on the shores of America in the year 1000 A.D., which is about 500 years prior to the landing of Christopher Columbus. The statue was a gift from the United States, honoring the 1930 Alþingi Millennial Festival, which commemorates the 1,000[th] anniversary of the Icelandic parliament's establishment in 930 A.D. at Þingvellir. Alexander Stirling Calder designed the statue.

- ### *Nauthólsvík Geothermal Beach*

Nauthólsvík geothermal beach is a golden-sanded geothermal beach in Reykjavík, which was opened in 2001. Tourists and local people alike are delighted to have such paradise in Reykjavík. In fact, it draws nearly 530,000 guests annually. Although the establishment of the geothermal beach was quite ambitious and extremely taxing, it became a successful project. It features a lagoon with huge sea walls in which hot geothermal water and cold sea merge and results in higher temperatures.

The primary goal of the geothermal beach's construction was to designate the Nauthólsvík bay as a haven for recreational activities as well as a great outdoor area for sea-swimming, sailing, and sunbathing. Sea swimming is enormously popular all throughout the year as people enjoy using the steam bath, hot tubs, and other shower facilities. Although the water drops below freezing point, people still come to Nauthólsvík for extreme activities dating back to the settlement age. Swimming in cold water might sound absurd, specifically in a country like Iceland; however, people, including residents and tourists of Reykjavík find the activity challenging and at the same time fulfilling. In 1030, Grettir Ásmundarson of the Icelandic Saga legend was recorded to have the oldest sea-swimming exploit, swimming across the bay in North Iceland to the Drangey Island with a distance of about 7 kilometers.

The temperature of the sea varies from -1.9 degrees during cold months to 17 degrees during summer. The average temperature ranges from 3 to 5 degrees during winter and 12 to 15 degrees during summer. Inside the lagoon, the sea temperature is higher during summer averaging from 15 o 19 degrees. This is due the geothermal heating. During winter, it is also warmer when the overspill from hot tubs reaches the lagoon. The temperatures may also vary depending on the tide. For instance, during high tide, the lagoon floods, causing the differences in the temperature.

- **The National Museum of Iceland**

The capital of Iceland is home to many fine museums but the National Museum of Iceland certainly outshines the rest. Within these walls, visitors are taken on a fascinating journey through the history and culture of this incredible country.

The exhibitions and displays at the National Museum are well laid out and illuminated, with a variety of temporary and permanent displays. The objects shown here range from various time periods, from the Viking era to modern times. There are more than two thousand objects showcased here from all over Iceland, but the highlights of the museum is undoubtedly the Valthjófsstadur door. Dating from the medieval period, it features exquisite carvings of scenes taken from the tale, *Le Chevalier au Lion*.

- **Einar Jonsson Museum**

Einar Jonsson (May 11th 1874 – October 18th 1954) was an Icelandic sculptor from the south and in 1909, he donated his beautiful works to the country providing that a museum was established to hold them. However, it wasn't until 1914 that the government accepted them; they donated 10,000 crowns for the construction of a museum, whilst another 20,000 crowns was raised and donated by private sources. Often referred to as Iceland's first sculptor, the people adored his work and the museum has long been a popular attraction.

Einar Jonsson picked the site where the museum was built – on Skolavorduhaed, on the outskirts of town – and was the first building to be constructed there. The sculptor designed the museum, and it is said that the building is his largest artwork.

- **Kopavogur Art Museum Gerdarsafn**

If you only have time to see one art museum when in Iceland, make sure it's this one. The Kopavogur Art Museum

Gerdarsafn is located within a beautiful building in Kopavogur in honor of the life and works of various artists, including the illustrious sculptor, Gerdur Helgadottir. Born in 1928, she rose to fame as the country's top modern sculptor, renowned for her exquisite stained glass (including those found in the windows of Kopavogur Church) and her mosaics.

In addition to works of Gerdur Helgadottir, the museum houses a wonderful collection of arts from Barbara Arnason and Valgerdur Briem, in addition to the private collections of Thorvaldur Gundmundsson. These beautiful collections can be found inside the museum's exhibitions and attract visitors from all over the world.

As well as displaying renowned artists' works, the museum also puts on exhibitions of works done by national artists, with around ten exhibitions held throughout the year. The museum has three exhibition halls, two of which can be found on the first floor, and the third on the ground floor.

- **Nordic House**

The Nordic House makes the top ten list of attractions in the capital every time and it isn't hard to see why. Inside, the museum houses an outstanding collection of artworks as well as hosting a wide range of cultural events and occasions. The building itself was created by the Finnish architect, Alvar Aalto (1898 – 1976) which boasts several of his signature features. Located around ten minutes away from the center of the city, Nordic House includes a library, an exceptional restaurant, exhibition halls and a concert hall, making it the place to go for cultural events.

In 2016, it was the 40th anniversary of Alvar Aalto's death, and so Nordic House honored his memory by creating a website featuring the top 15 buildings he designed over the years. He had designed 500, with 300 being constructed, with the Nordic House being prominent on the website.

The restaurant within Nordic House is famous across Iceland. Master chef, Sveinn Kjartansson, has been presenting shows on television how to create mouth-watering dishes using local ingredients and today, visitors can sample some of his signature dishes at the restaurant.

In addition to all of this, the museum houses a different cultural event each day, whether its theatre, music, art or dance performances.

- **Reykjavík Art Museum**

Also known as Kjarvalsstaðir, the Reykjavik Art Museum was the first museum in the country planned to showcase various types of modern art. The museum opened its doors to the public in 1973 and took its name from Johannes S. Kjarval (1885 – 1972), a renowned painter, one of the country's most prominent artists of all time. The museum houses a superb collection of his works in a year-round exhibition.

The museum boasts a wide collection of paintings, sculptures and other works from the country's top artists. Spread out over three buildings, it also features works from artists from all over the world.

Each year, the Reykjavik Art Museum hosts roughly twenty exhibitions and shows in addition to the temporary and permanent displays here. You will see everything from the traditional to contemporary and even works that could push the boundaries, making it a fantastic place to explore.

- **The Living Art Museum**

The Living Art Museum, also known as Nylo, is one of the most important museums dedicated to showcasing contemporary art within the nation's capital. Not only does it present art created by Icelandic artists, it also displays those done by international painters, sculptors and other visual artists. The museum is managed by artists and is a non-profit organization, with artists themselves raising the capital needed to fund the museum. Over the years, they have gained a reputation for showcasing work that pushes the boundaries, putting on thought provoking exhibitions and raising awareness in the art community.

- **The National Archives**

As can be imagined by the name, the National Archives is where the archives of the Icelandic people and its government are stored. It's not really a museum as such, but visitors can explore the archives and look in the old books and other texts. If you are tracing family or lineage in Iceland, then the National Archives has a great resource center, located within the Reading Room.

- **Numismatic Museum**

For those who are interested in money and coins, then the Numismatic Museum is the ideal place to visit. The museum houses a fantastic array of Icelandic and international coins and paper money, all from various times in history.

The museum boasts a collection of around 20,000 coins and around 5,000 notes. Some of these can be found on display within the Central Bank in Kalkofnsvegur.

Where to Eat in Reykjavík

- ***101 Restaurant and Bar***

The chic 101 Restaurant and Bar is situated on the ground floor of the 101 Hotel. It offers a unique menu for lunch and dinner as well as perfect cocktail refreshments. Its kitchen opens daily from 7 in the morning until 11 in the evening. Breakfast is offered from 7 until 10:30 in the morning during weekdays and 7 until 11 in the morning during weekends. The Bar is open until midnight during weekdays and 1 in the morning during weekends.

- ***Hressingarskalinn***

Hressingarskalinn is situated in the center of Reykjavík. It is a bistro-style restaurant and bar that offers wide-ranging menu. Guests also enjoy its free Internet access while having fund with the restaurant's live music. Hressingarskalinn is a popular place for hanging out during the day with its lively atmosphere, especially during weekends. It features a garden, which is popular during summer for its party atmosphere.

- ***Slipp Bar***

Travelers and tourists can enjoy and experience the life in Reykjavík just like a local in the Slipp Bar. It is situated at the Iceland Air Hotel Reykjavík Marina. It features exciting and Icelandic events, including stand-up comedy, arts, and music. It is also a place where old and new friends can gather over a drink. Its drink menu features a selection of cocktails and wine, which will truly amaze those who love to drink. In addition, it also offers zesty yet affordable food any time of the day. Slipp Bar has a trendy interior that guests feel comfortable with. It also offers majestic views of both the mountains and the great sea. Slipp Bar is also popular among tourists as it is near the Reykjavík Dry Dock.

Where to Stay in Reykjavík

- ### *101 Hotel*

A member of Design Hotels, 101 Hotel is a boutique accommodation located at the center of Reykjavík's downtown. It is near the Icelandic Opera House, cafes, restaurants, businesses, and shops. Thus, it is a perfect place to stay for travelers and visitors who want everything in just one area.

For booking inquiries and prices, interested parties can visit www.101hotel.is.

- ### *Hotel Phoenix*

Hotel Phoenix is a privately owned hotel, which is situated in Laugavegur the main shopping street in Reykjavík. Although the hotel is quite small, its 9 rooms are extremely spacious. In addition, the hotel features modern amenities as well as private facilities.

Interested parties may visit www.phoenix.is for booking information and prices.

- ### *Hotel Laxnes*

Hotel Laxnes is situated opposite a river and overlooks the mountain of Esja. It is also next to waterfalls, rivers, a beautiful lake, sea, and mountains, making it an ideal place for nature lovers and hikers. Guests also have the chance to view the Northern lights from the hotel.

Hotel Laxnes is only 10 minutes away from the center of Reykjavík. It resembles a fairytale world although it is a modern country style hotel lodge. It also has a view of the mountain in the Mosfellsbaer area.

Hotel Laxnes is popular for featuring the best of city life and country living. It is close to some of the city's attractions and destinations, including Laxnes horse riding, fishing lake, Alafoss Viking Wool store, and golf course. It is also in proximity with the famous Golden Circle trip. At the Laxnes Hotel, guests will truly experience both city and country life.

Hotel Laxnes has 26 large modern rooms. It offers twin and double rooms as well as studio and family rooms for those who come in groups. The guest rooms are spacious and decorated in a functional style. All of the rooms in Hotel Laxnes are equipped with private bathrooms, access to on-site parking and free Internet access.

Interested parties may visit their website www.hotellaxnes.is for booking information and rates.

Chapter 7 – Icelandic Cuisine

Sampling the local cuisine is part and parcel of travel. Food and drink is a great way of getting to know the local culture and Iceland is no exception. The country boasts a wide range of delectable dishes – some which may be considered a little strange to some – all using local ingredients.

Iceland is renowned for its clean environment, which allows food products to grow healthy, resulting in mouth-wateringly fresh dishes. When visiting Iceland, you can try a variety of traditional foods; from mountain lamb to freshly caught cod to locally sourced goats cheese. Take a look at some of the great dishes just waiting for you.

Icelandic Mountain Lamb

Mountain lamb is the Must Try dish when in Iceland. Over the summer months, sheep are allowed to feast on wild berries, herbs and anything else they can get their jaws around. As a result, all the tastiness of the countryside comes through their own delicious meat, with numerous international chefs praising it. The best time to try Icelandic Mountain Lamb is during autumn when the sheep are brought in from the wilderness and housed safely for the winter. Hangikjot is basically smoked lamb and is especially enjoyed at the Christmas period.

Fish, Fish and More Fish

D. H. Lawrence wrote in Whales Weep Not, *“They say the sea is cold, but the sea contains the hottest blood of all, and the wildest, the most urgent”* and he certainly wasn't wrong. The

Atlantic Ocean may be cold but it is teeming with a variety of fresh fish and marine creatures. Fresh seafood features in many different types of Icelandic dishes and can be purchased from supermarkets only a few hours after being caught.

The most popular types of fish you will find are cod, herring, halibut, trout and salmon. Langoustine lobster is regularly fished off the coast of Hofn in the south, and prawns and mussels from the northern regions. Seafood dishes are plentiful and reasonable for the budget conscious. For salmon lovers, the fish is typically smoked and comes with a herb sauce. Cod is usually found in soups.

Dairy Products

Iceland produces a range of dairy products that rivals Mountain Lamb when it comes to tastiness. As with lamb, milk, cheese, yogurts and other dairy products are produced without any antibiotics or anything else. Just 100% natural ingredients. Skyr is the number one dairy product in the country; it looks similar to Greek yoghurt but it is, in fact, a type of soft cheese. Locals typically eat it at breakfast, as snacks and as desserts since it has an abundance of calcium and has low amounts of calories.

Cheese is another popular dairy product. In fact, Iceland produces over 100 different types. The majority of these are mild in taste and can be similar in texture to Gouda, but the most popular cheeses on the island is blue cheese. For those who have a sweet tooth, Icelandic ice cream is rich and creamy and can purchased on the farms themselves.

Fresh Fruits and Vegetables

Iceland is not generally considered a 'fruit country' due to the colder weather. However, much of the country's fruits and vegetables are grown within greenhouses, which are heated by natural hot springs. Most of these greenhouses can be found in the south and are pesticide free and organic. As soon as you bite into it, you can really taste the difference. There is a definite crisp and a deeper flavor to Iceland's different fruits and vegetables than what you would find in the supermarkets back home.

Hakarl

There are several delicacies, which are traditionally eaten in Iceland, dating back to the time of the Vikings. Out of them all, hakarl is the most famous. Hakarl is basically fermented Greenland shark. The meat is deadly if you consume it fresh but it was discovered that if it was buried for over three months, the meat became edible, if a bit tough and rubbery. Hakarl is eaten with a typical liquor called Brennivin and consumed between January and February during the Thorrablot Viking Food Festival where other traditional delicacies are eaten.

Kjötsúpa (Meat soup)

Kjötsúpa, or meat soup, is another popular lamb dish, although it generally features the tough lamb meat but you can use any meat you wish. Lamb is diced into small chunks and placed over a stove with a variety of other ingredients – such as rice, carrots and onions – for a long period before enjoying.

However, locals say that Kjötsúpa is tastier if you allow it to sit for 24 hours before heating it up again.

Ein með öllu

Ein með öllu is basically the Icelandic version of the American hot dog but uses lamb instead of whatever is used in the American version (do *you* know what's inside them?), but the sauce makes it so much better. When you order a Ein með öllu, get it with everything – tomato sauce, a brownish colored mustard, both raw and fried onions and a sauce consisting of relish and mayonnaise.

Svið

Svið means 'singed' in Icelandic and refers to the process of removing the hair from the head of a sheep. After singing, the brains are removed from sheep's head and then boiled for several hours. It is generally served with potatoes, vegetables and a jelly-like consistency made from rhubarb. Those who order this traditional meal are expected to eat everything, including the eyes. Although it may turn your stomach at the very thought, Svið is a delicious meal and a must try when visiting Iceland.

Conclusion

Once again thank you for choosing *Lost Travelers*!

I hope we were able to provide you with the best travel tips when visiting Iceland.

And we hope you enjoy your travels.

"Travel Brings Power and Love Back To Your Life"

- Rumi

Finally, if you enjoyed this guide, then I'd like to ask you for a favor, would you be kind enough to leave a review for this book on Amazon? It'd be greatly appreciated!

- Simply search the keywords "Iceland Travel Guide" on Amazon or go to our Author page "Lost Travelers" to review.

Please know that your satisfaction is important to us. If you were not happy with the book, please email us with the reason so we may serve you more accordingly next time.

- Email: info@losttravelers.com

Thank you and good luck!

NOTES

NOTES

NOTES

NOTES

Preview Of 'New Zealand: The Ultimate New Zealand Travel Guide By A Traveler For A Traveler

Located 2,012 km to the south of Australia is New Zealand. There are two main islands comprising it, the North and South islands, and outlying islands scattered within the vicinity. Its two main islands are separated by a body of water known as the Cook Strait. The North Island is 829 km long. Its southern end is volcanic and because of this, there are plenty of excellent hot springs and geysers in the area. On the South island, lies the Southern Alps by the west end. Here is where one will find the highest point in New Zealand which is Mount Cook. It is 12,316 feet tall!

Some of the outlying islands are inhabited while others are not. The inhabited islands include Chatham, Great Barrier, and Stewart islands. The largest of the uninhabited islands are Campbell, Kermadec, Antipodes, and Auckland islands.

The first inhabitants of New Zealand were the Maoris. Their initial population was only 1,000 people. According to their oral history, it took the initial Maori population seven canoes to reach New Zealand from other parts of Polynesia. It was in the mid-1600s that the island cluster was explored by a man named Abel Tasma, a Dutch navigator. Another foreigner, a British by the name of James Cook, engaged in three voyages to New Zealand the first one taking place in 1769. New Zealand became a formal annex to Britain during the mid 1800s.

During this time, the Treaty of Waitangi was signed between Britain and the Maoris. It stated that there will be ample protection for Maori land should the Maoris accept British rule. Despite the treaty, tension between both factions intensified over time due to the continuous encroachment by British settlers.

Check out the rest of New Zealand: The Ultimate New Zealand Travel Guide on Amazon by simply searching it.

Check Out Our Other Books

Below you'll find some of our other popular books that are on Amazon and Kindle as well. Simply search the titles below to check them out. Alternatively, you can visit our author page (Lost Travelers) on Amazon to see other work done by us.

- Vienna: The Ultimate Vienna Travel Guide By A Traveler For A Traveler

- Barcelona: The Ultimate Barcelona Travel Guide By A Traveler For A Traveler

- London: The Ultimate London Travel Guide By A Traveler For A Traveler

- Istanbul: The Ultimate Istanbul Travel Guide By A Traveler For A Traveler

- Vietnam: The Ultimate Vietnam Travel Guide By A Traveler For A Traveler

- Peru: The Ultimate Peru Travel Guide By A Traveler For A Traveler

- Australia: The Ultimate Australia Guide By A Traveler For A Traveler

- Japan: The Ultimate Japan Travel Guide By A Traveler For A Traveler

- New Zealand: The Ultimate New Zealand Travel Guide By A Traveler For A Traveler

- Dublin: The Ultimate Dublin Travel Guide By A Traveler For A Traveler

- Thailand: The Ultimate Thailand Travel Guide By A Traveler For A Traveler

- Iceland: The Ultimate Iceland Travel Guide By A Traveler For A Traveler

- Santorini: The Ultimate Santorini Travel Guide By A Traveler For A Traveler

- Italy: The Ultimate Italy Travel Guide By A Traveler For A Traveler

You can easily search for these titles on the Amazon website to find them.

Made in the USA
Coppell, TX
21 April 2023

15902586R00066